A Journey Through
SPACE

by Steve Parker

Illustrated by John Haslam

Copyright © Marshall Editions 2015
Part of The Quarto Group
The Old Brewery, 6 Blundell Street,
London, N7 9BH

First published in the UK in 2015 by QED Publishing

A catalogue record for this book is available from the British Library.

ISBN 978 1 78493 298 5 (hardback edition)

Publisher: Zeta Jones
Associate Publisher: Maxime Boucknooghe
Art Director: Susi Martin
Managing Editor: Laura Knowles
Production: Nikki Ingram
Consultant: David Hawksett

Originated in Hong Kong by Cypress Colours (HK) Ltd
Printed and bound in China by Toppan Leefung Printing Ltd.

10 9 8 7 6 5 4 3 2 1   15 16 17 18 19

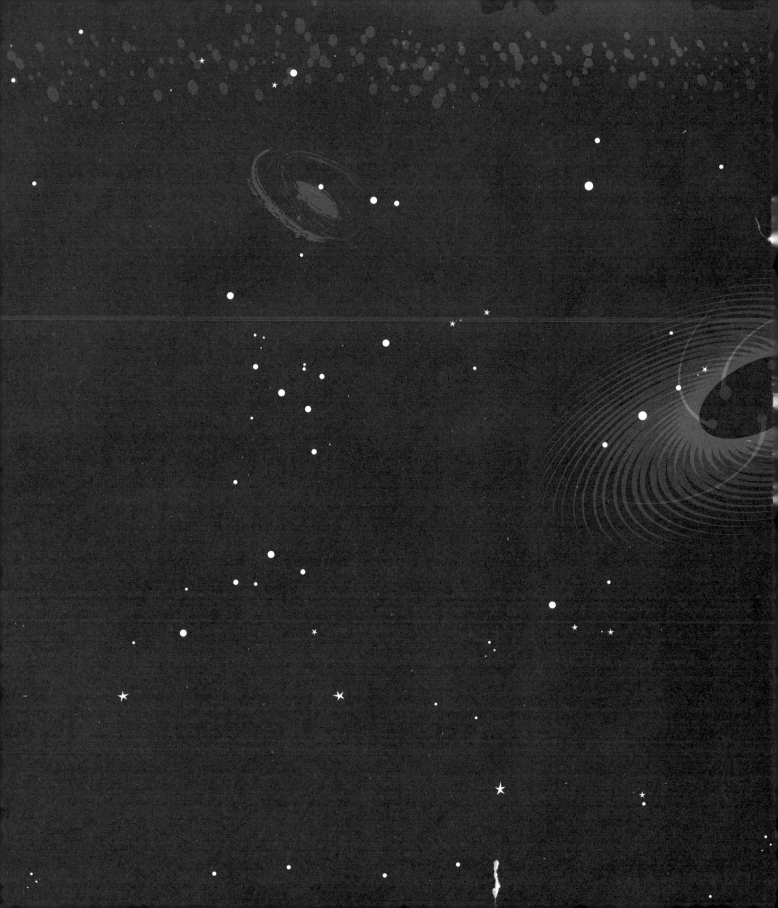

Contents

Let's begin our journey

Have you ever looked up at the night sky and wondered what it would be like to zoom through space? It's so far away, but there are so many amazing sights to see...

Wow! A thousand times bigger!

6

Stargazing

As the Sun sets, the Moon and stars come out. So do the people who study them. These people are called astronomers. They use telescopes to look at space. Telescopes make faraway objects seem much closer.

Some telescopes are as big as the astronomers. Some telescopes are bigger than 100 houses! They make things look over a thousand times bigger than they really are.

Blast off!

The only way to journey into space is in a rocket, also called a launch vehicle. It has the most powerful engines in the world.

Some rockets carry machines such as satellites and robot-like space probes. Some carry spacecraft with people, called astronauts. It takes months to get ready. Everything is checked many times.

5 4 3 2 1

The people at the control centre begin
the countdown. Five, four, three, two, one…
Flames blast out of the end of the rocket.
We have lift-off!

As the rocket takes off, the ground shakes.
At first the rocket goes slowly. In one
minute, it is faster than a jet plane, and in
another few minutes, 25 times faster.

Blast off!

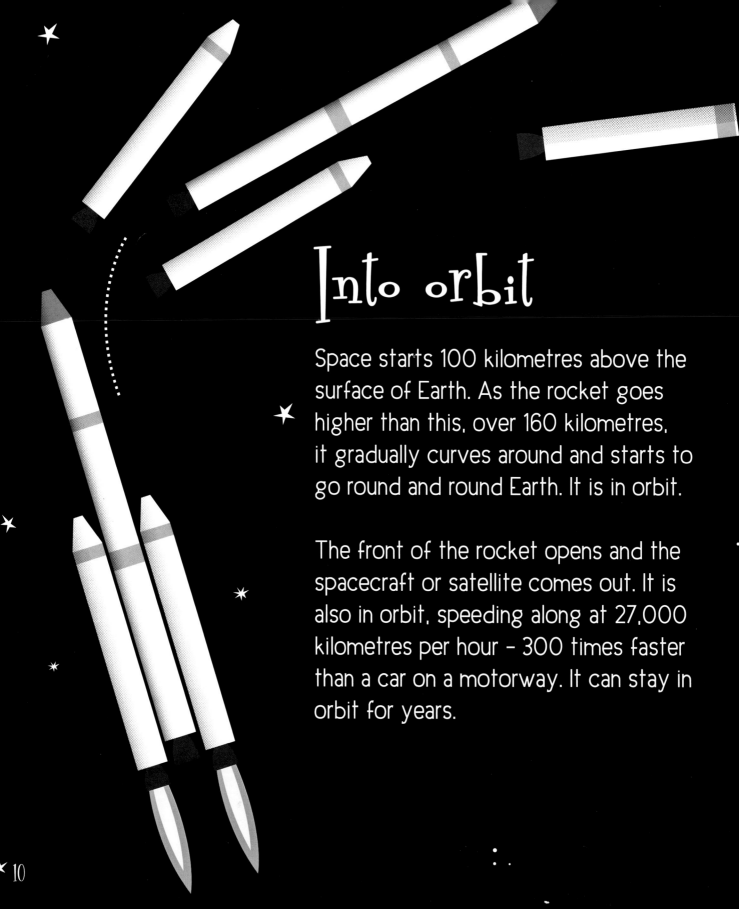

Into orbit

Space starts 100 kilometres above the surface of Earth. As the rocket goes higher than this, over 160 kilometres, it gradually curves around and starts to go round and round Earth. It is in orbit.

The front of the rocket opens and the spacecraft or satellite comes out. It is also in orbit, speeding along at 27,000 kilometres per hour – 300 times faster than a car on a motorway. It can stay in orbit for years.

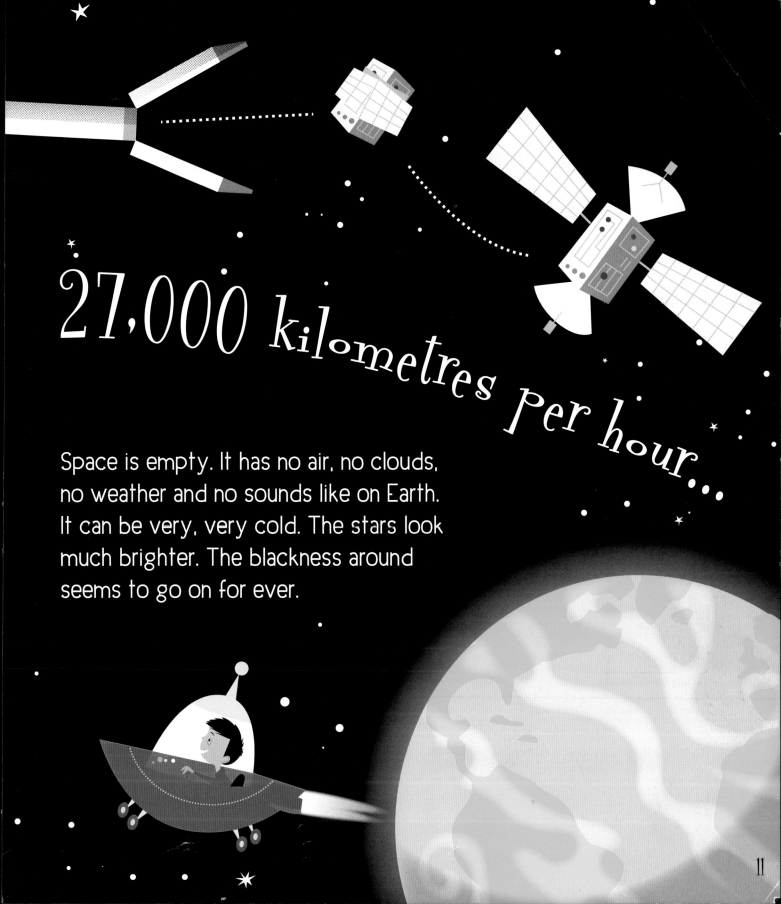

27,000 kilometres per hour...

Space is empty. It has no air, no clouds, no weather and no sounds like on Earth. It can be very, very cold. The stars look much brighter. The blackness around seems to go on for ever.

Living in space

Something in orbit around Earth, or another space object, is called a satellite. The first satellite was Sputnik 1, in 1957 – around 60 years ago. It was about the same size as a beach ball.

Sputnik

The Hubble Space Telescope is the size of a school bus. It was launched more than 25 years ago. It has taken many amazing pictures of deep space.

The biggest satellite is the ISS, the International Space Station. It would cover a football pitch. Astronauts live here for weeks, even months.

Inside the Space Station, astronauts and everything else float about, with no weight. Wouldn't that be a strange feeling!

Hubble Space Telescope

ISS

The Moon

The Moon is the nearest thing to
us in space that is really huge. It is
one-quarter as wide as Earth. It takes
three days to get there.

From Earth, the Moon seems to change
shape. But that is just the way sunlight
shines on it. The parts with no sunlight
look black.

Vrooom!

The Moon has rocky mountains, wide flat areas of dusty ground, and bowl-shaped craters. It has no air and no life.

The first two astronauts landed on the Moon in 1969, in the spacecraft Apollo 11. Over the next few years, another 10 astronauts visited the Moon. The last two went in 1972, and drove a special electric car called a lunar rover.

384,000 kilometres from Earth

The Sun

Stars are huge space objects that give out light and heat. Looking up from Earth at night time, the dark sky twinkles with thousands of distant stars.

By day, there is one star that is very near, bright and hot. It is a giant ball of flames and fire – the Sun.

Never look

More than one million Earths could
fit inside the Sun. At the surface it
is 6,000 degrees Celsius, which is
25 times hotter than a home oven.

Massive flames leap up from the
Sun's surface, curl around and
back in. Slightly darker, cooler
patches are known as sunspots.
Most last only a few days.

straight at the Sun — it can really harm your eyes

The inner planets

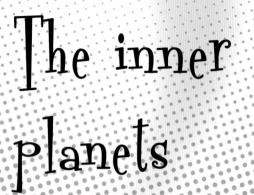

Mercury

Earth is one of eight planets that go around, or orbit, the Sun. The nearest planet to the Sun is Mercury, and next is Venus.

Mercury is the smallest planet, only one-third as wide as Earth. It is also hotter than an oven. It takes 88 days to go around the Sun. (Earth takes 365 days, which is one year.)

The space probe MESSENGER went around Mercury. As big as an office desk, it took pictures and measured temperatures – then it ran out of fuel and crashed into the planet.

Venus is the closest planet to Earth and it is about the same size. It takes 225 days to orbit the Sun. It is covered with thick clouds of poisonous acids. Underneath are tall mountains and deep valleys.

The Venus Express space probe orbited Venus for nine years. It took thousands of measurements. Then it fell into the deadly clouds and burned up.

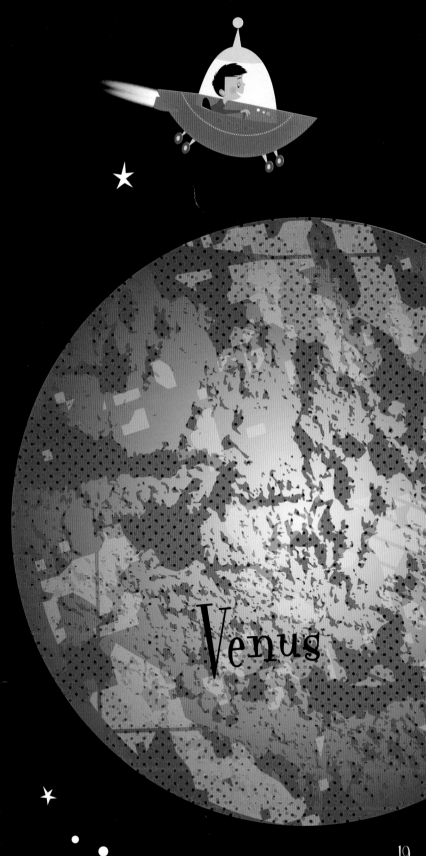

Venus

Mars

Zooming past Earth, the next planet from the Sun is Mars. It is known as the 'Red Planet' because its rocks and dust are mostly red-brown. Mars is half as wide as Earth and takes 687 days to go around the Sun.

Mars has air and winds. But the air is too thin and harmful for people to breathe. So far, no astronauts have been there.

More than 25 spacecraft have journeyed to Mars, and seven landed on the surface. Most of these landers looked for signs of life. They have not found any – yet.

Landers with wheels are called rovers. Three rovers the size of small cars have been put on Mars. They made many discoveries. Two rovers, called Opportunity and Curiosity, are still going.

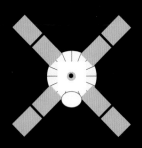

Mars

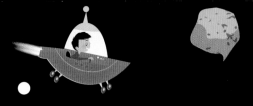

Asteroids

As well as planets, there are also smaller objects going around the Sun. They are called asteroids. Most of them are between Mars and the next furthest planet, Jupiter.

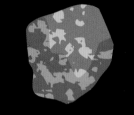

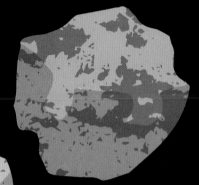

Like planets and moons, asteroids do not make any light. They are seen because sunlight shines on them. Most are lumpy, like potatoes.

The biggest asteroid is Ceres, which is almost 1,000 kilometres long. Next in size is Vesta, which is about half as big. The smallest asteroids are only the size of cars.

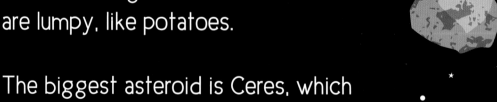

Jupiter

Going around Ceres is the DAWN space probe. It was sent from Earth and visited Vesta on its way to Ceres.

Giant planets

Planets near the Sun, like Earth, are mainly solid rock. The four distant planets are like huge balls of gas and liquid spinning in space. They are known as gas giants.

Jupiter is the biggest planet. It is 11 times wider than Earth. It also spins the fastest, once every 10 hours. (Earth spins once in 24 hours.) Jupiter's storm, the Great Red Spot, is three times bigger than Earth!

Jupiter

Great Red Spot

Saturn is nine times wider than Earth. It has beautiful rings made of lumps of rock and ice, and 62 moons – more than any other planet. In 2004 the Cassini-Huygens space probe visited Saturn and landed on one of its moons, Titan.

Saturn

The outer planets

Uranus

Uranus is blue-green and icy-cold. It takes 84 years to go around the Sun, and is four times wider than Earth.

Neptune is blue and similar in size to Uranus. It is the furthest planet and takes 165 years to orbit the Sun. It also has the strongest winds. They blow at 2,000 kilometres per hour – five times faster than hurricanes on Earth.

In 1977 the space probe Voyager 2 left Earth. Over many years, its vast journey took it past all four outer planets, including Neptune. No other space probe has visited Uranus and Neptune since.

Neptune

The solar system

The Sun and its orbiting planets, moons and asteroids are all called the solar system. At the outer edge of the solar system are many more strange objects. These include dwarf planets and comets.

The New Horizons probe

Dwarf planets are all much smaller than Earth. Even the biggest two, Eris and Pluto, are smaller than our Moon.

It takes Pluto 248 years to go once around the Sun. Dwarf planets in this part of the solar system are so far away from the Sun that, if you could visit one and look out into space, the Sun would look like almost any other small, twinkling star.

took nine years to reach Pluto.

New Horizons

Pluto

Comets

Comets are small, ice-cold objects that come from the furthest parts of our solar system. As they journey towards the Sun, they warm up. The solid lumpy part, called the nucleus, makes a long, bright tail.

The comet loops around the Sun. Its tail does not trail behind but always points away from the Sun. Then it travels away again, cold and dark. Perhaps it will return years later.

Philae lander

In 2014, after a 10-year journey, the car-sized Rosetta space probe became the first to orbit a comet. Rosetta took many amazing pictures and its small lander, Philae, touched down onto the surface.

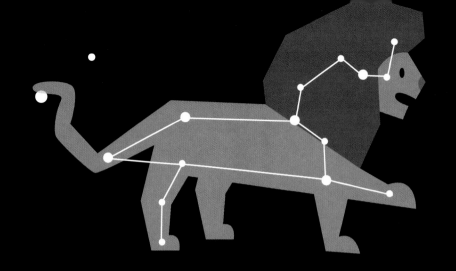

Shapes in the stars

Long ago, people looked up at the stars and imagined that their patterns made shapes, like animals and buildings. These shapes were called constellations and people gave them many names.

Today, there are 88 constellations, each in a different part of the sky.

The biggest constellation is Hydra, the Snake.
Its bright stars form a long, winding shape.
The smallest constellation is Crux, the Cross.
Four of its main stars make a cross.

In Leo, the Lion, the brighter stars make a
shape like a prowling lion. In Ursa Major, the
Great Bear, seven bright stars form a pattern
called the Plough or Big Dipper.

Our galaxy

Stars and their planets are not spread evenly through space. They are in huge groups called galaxies. Each galaxy has hundreds of billions of stars. It is separated from other galaxies by empty space.

Our solar system is in a galaxy called the Milky Way. Seen from here on Earth, its stars show up as a faint pale band across the night sky.

The Milky Way contains more than 200 billion stars. The Sun and its planets, and us, are about halfway between the centre of the galaxy and its edge.

The Milky Way is a spiral galaxy...

...from the outside, it looks like this!

Moving in space

Nothing in space is still. Earth and other planets spin around, and they orbit the Sun. The Sun is going around the centre of its Milky Way galaxy. Each orbit takes a long time – about 230 million years!

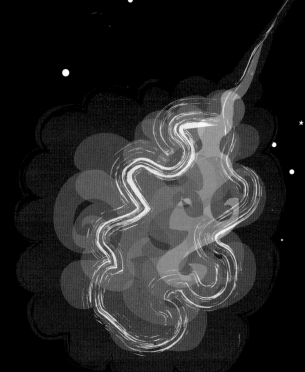

The Milky Way is also flying through space at incredible speed, hundreds of kilometres every second. There are billions of other galaxies, all speeding through space too. Most are moving away from each other and getting further apart.

Some galaxies are flat like plates. Some are egg-shaped. Some are round balls or rings. Some have no shape at all.

Strange space

A journey into deepest space goes past some very strange things. Not even space experts know all about them.

A neutron star is tiny, probably only 16 kilometres across. It does not give out much light, but it is very heavy. One spoonful of it would weigh more than a mountain on Earth.

In the middle of most galaxies is a black hole. It may be a few kilometres across, or thousands of kilometres. But it cannot be seen. It contains so many stars squashed together that its pull of gravity is huge. Even light cannot get out.

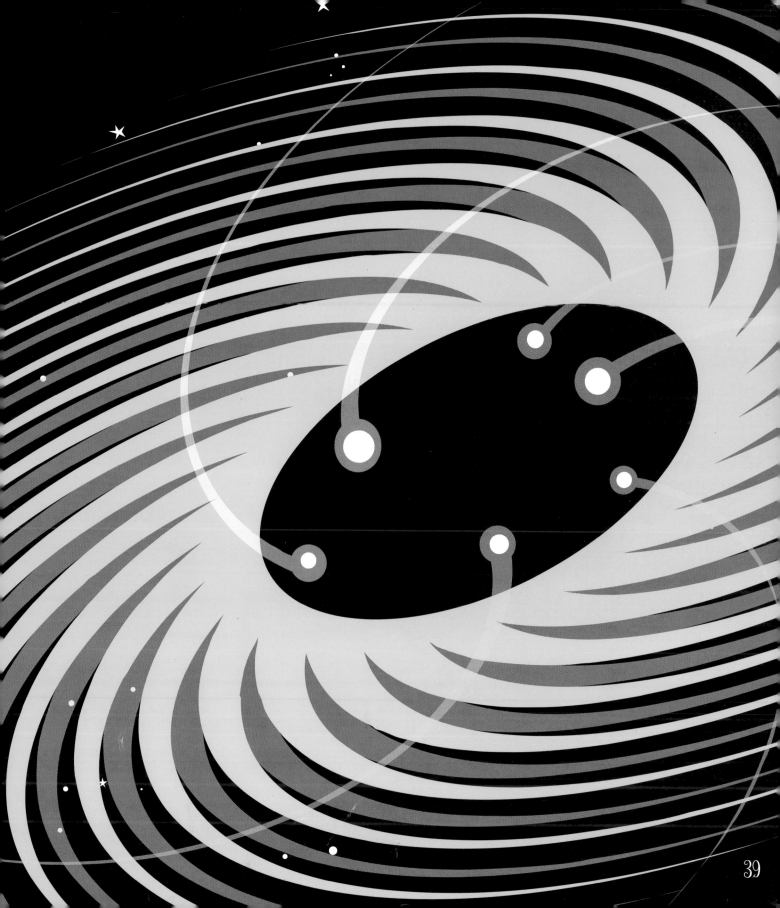

Across the universe

The universe is all of space, and everything in it – planets, stars, galaxies, black holes and the rest.

No one really knows the shape or size of the universe. It could be round like a ball, curved like a dome, or ring-shaped. Some space experts think it is flat – like a sandwich!

The universe started 13,800 million years ago. At first it was a tiny spot with everything squeezed into it.

Then BOOM! – the Big Bang happened. The universe started to get bigger. Stars and other space objects formed. The universe is still getting bigger today. It will probably keep growing for billions of years, maybe even forever.

Longest journey

The furthest that people have travelled into space is the Moon. The next place, in many years' time, may be the planet Mars.

Going to Mars will need a very big, powerful rocket. It will have to go much faster than today's rockets. It must carry food, water and everything else the astronauts need – even their air!

The journey to Mars will take six months. Then a few weeks on the planet. Plus another six months to come back. Imagine a birthday party in space!

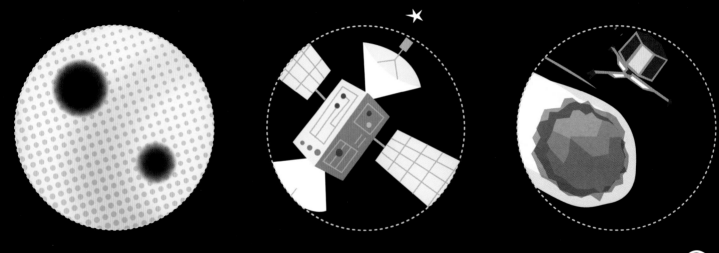

Can you spot these space objects?

Can you work out what they are?

Quiz time!

Can you answer these questions about the solar system? Here's a hint – you can find all the answers in this book.

1. How many planets go round the Sun?

2. Which planet is closest to Earth?

3. What is the name of Jupiter's giant storm?

4. What did astronauts drive around in on the Moon?

5. Have any astronauts visited Mars?

6. What is the name of the biggest constellation?

Answers

1. Eight, 2. Venus, 3. The Great
Red Spot, 4. The lunar rover,
5. No – nobody has gone to
Mars...yet, 6. Hydra (the Snake),
7. The Milky Way, 8. Blue.

8. What colour is
the planet Neptune?

7. What is the name
of our galaxy?

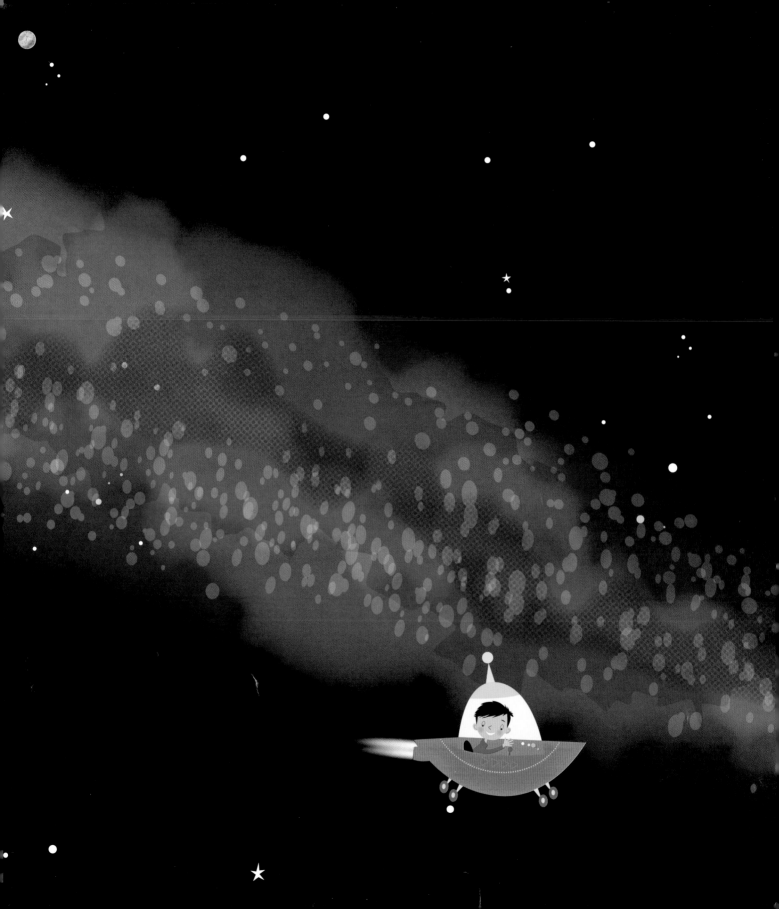